Dec 2019

COOL
PAPER ART

PAPERMAKING

HANDMADE PAPER AND PAPER PRODUCTS

MEGAN
BORGERT-SPANIOL

Checkerboard
Library

An Imprint of Abdo Publishing
abdobooks.com

abdobooks.com

Published by Abdo Publishing, a division of ABDO, PO Box 398166, Minneapolis, Minnesota 55439. Copyright © 2020 by Abdo Consulting Group, Inc. International copyrights reserved in all countries. No part of this book may be reproduced in any form without written permission from the publisher. Checkerboard Library™ is a trademark and logo of Abdo Publishing.

Printed in the United States of America, North Mankato, Minnesota
052019
092019

THIS BOOK CONTAINS
RECYCLED MATERIALS

Design: Christa Schneider, Mighty Media, Inc.
Production: Mighty Media, Inc.
Editor: Liz Salzmann
Cover Photographs: Mighty Media, Inc.
Interior Photographs: Mighty Media, Inc., pp. 1, 3, 4 (pattern), 7 (top), 8 (middle), 9–10, 11 (pattern, stapler, mesh, scissors, ruler, blender), 12–27 (all), 28 (pattern), 30, 31, 32; Shutterstock Images, pp. 4–5, 5, 6 (both), 7 (bottom), 8 (top, bottom), 11 (frame), 28 (book), 29

The following manufacturers/names appearing in this book are trademarks: Mod Podge®, Osterizer®, Stanley® Bostitch®

Library of Congress Control Number: 2018966251

Publisher's Cataloging-in-Publication Data
Names: Borgert-Spaniol, Megan, author.
Title: Papermaking: handmade paper and paper products / by Megan Borgert-Spaniol
Other title: Handmade paper and paper products
Description: Minneapolis, Minnesota : Abdo Publishing, 2020 | Series: Cool paper art | Includes online resources and index.
Identifiers: ISBN 9781532119477 (lib. bdg.) | ISBN 9781532173936 (ebook
Subjects: LCSH: Paper art--Juvenile literature. | Papermaking--Juvenile literature. | Paper products--Juvenile literature. | Crafts (Handicrafts)--Juvenile literature.
Classification: DDC 676.22--dc23

CONTENTS

PAPERMAKING

How often do you use paper? Probably every day. You draw pictures and write school reports on paper. You also use paper when you read books, buy movie tickets, and more. That's a lot of paper!

Before paper, people wrote on materials such as bark, silk, leather, and bamboo. Then, nearly 2,000 years ago, Chinese court official Cai Lun created a lighter, cheaper material. It was made of rags and plant fibers that had been soaked, pressed into sheets, and dried. It was the first paper.

Soon, papermaking spread from China all across the world. Over time, papermakers discovered new and better methods for making paper.

Today, most paper is produced in factories by machines. However, craftspeople around the world have continued to make paper by hand. And with just a few basic materials, you can make handmade paper too!

MATERIALS & BASICS

Even with the help of machines, the papermaking process is still similar to that of 2,000 years ago. First, plant fibers are beaten and soaked in water. This creates paper **pulp**. Then, the pulp is filtered through a mold to form a sheet. Finally, the wet sheet is pressed and dried.

FIBERS

To make your own paper, you'll first need fibers for your paper pulp. Like **traditional** papermakers, you can use plants. These include:

- **grasses**
- **leaves**
- **stems**

You can also make paper **pulp** with the fibers of existing paper products. These include:

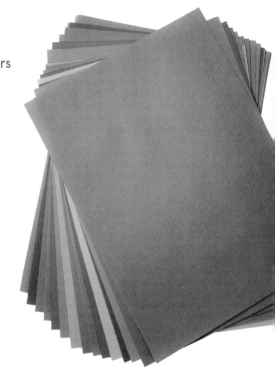

- **card stock**
- **construction paper**
- **napkins**
- **paper towels**
- **tissue paper**

Most projects in this book use recycled papers to make paper pulp. These include:

- **cardboard**
- **junk mail**
- **magazines**
- **newspapers**
- **paper bags**

Whatever fiber you use, you'll need to cut it into smaller pieces. Running paper through a paper shredder is a quick, easy way to do this. Or you can use scissors to cut the paper into thin strips. If using plant material, cut it into pieces about the size of a quarter.

PAPER PULP

Once you have prepared your fibers, it's time to add water. This will break the fibers down into a **pulp**. There are several different ways to make paper pulp. The projects in this book show three of these methods.

SHAKING

This works well for paper fibers that break down easily, such as newspaper or tissue paper.

SOAKING AND BLENDING

This works well for tougher paper fibers, such as junk mail or cardboard.

SOAKING, BOILING, AND BLENDING

This works well for plant fibers, which do not break down easily.

PAPER MOLDS

When your paper **pulp** is ready, you'll need a mold to form your paper. Some papermakers use a tool called a mold and deckle. The mold is the filter that catches the fibers in paper pulp. This separates the fibers from the water. The deckle is a frame around the edges of a mold. This shapes the fibers into a sheet.

To make your own mold with a built-in deckle:

1. Remove the backing board and glass from a picture frame.

2. Cut a piece of **mesh** with the same dimensions as the picture frame.

3. Staple the mesh to the back of the picture frame. Be sure to staple all around the edges so the mesh is secure.

TOOLS & SUPPLIES

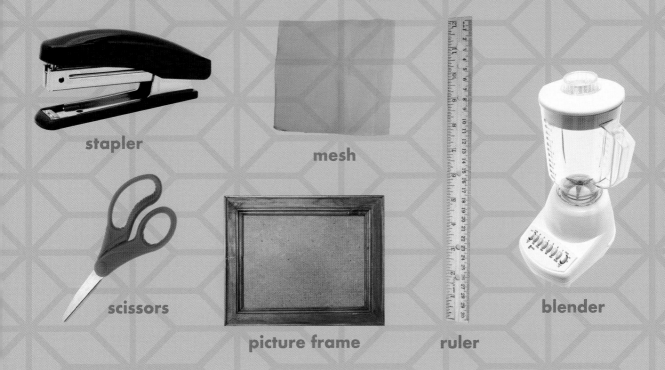

stapler

mesh

scissors

picture frame

ruler

blender

TIPS & TRICKS

You can use an old window screen as a mold and lay a frame on top of it for a deckle. And you don't always have to use a deckle. Instead, pour the **pulp** on the mold and shape it with your fingers.

PAPERMAKING METHODS

You've made your paper **pulp** and paper mold. Now you're finally ready to make paper! The projects in this book show three different methods of making paper.

PREP & POUR

Set the mold in a plastic tub. Pour the paper pulp onto the mold. Spread the pulp in an even layer.

TIPS & TRICKS

Do you plan to write on your paper with a pen? If so, stir or blend 2 teaspoons of liquid starch into the paper pulp. This will keep ink from bleeding into the paper when you write on it.

DIP & LIFT

Pour the **pulp** into a plastic tub. Dip the mold into the tub at an angle. Move the mold back and forth in the pulp to evenly **distribute** pulp on the mold. Keep the mold level as you lift it from the tub. Let any extra water drain into the tub.

STRAIN & SCOOP

Pour the pulp into a strainer to remove the extra water. Scoop up some pulp with your hand and press it onto the mold. This method is best suited for making paper bowls or other crafts besides flat sheets.

HANDMADE PAPER ART

Handmade paper art doesn't have to come from handmade paper. You can make all kinds of cool items out of new, used, or recycled paper. This book shows you how to turn used or recycled paper into a handmade gift bag. But you can also use paper to make handmade journals, pencil holders, gift boxes, and more!

QUICK SHAKE PAPER

- medium jar with lid
- shredded paper
- shredded colored tissue paper
- water
- mold
- plastic tub
- towel
- hair dryer
- fork
- decorating supplies

1
Fill the jar about halfway with shredded paper.

2
Add shredded colored tissue paper until the jar is nearly full.

3
Fill the jar with enough warm water to cover the paper. Screw the lid on tightly.

4

Shake the jar continuously for about ten minutes. Stop shaking when the color is **distributed** evenly and the paper is broken down into small bits.

5

Use the prep & pour method to fill the mold (see page 12).

6

Remove the mold from the tub. Press a towel on the **pulp** to soak up any extra water. Then blow on each side of the mold with a hair dryer for about five minutes.

7

Gently poke the paper with a fork through the **mesh**. This will loosen the paper from the mesh.

8

Once the paper is free from the mesh, lift the mold off of the paper. Let the paper dry completely. Use decorating supplies to turn your homemade paper into a greeting card, invitation, or other craft!

BITS OF NATURE PAPER

- shredded paper
- large bowl
- water
- blender
- plastic tub
- bits of nature (small leaves, flower petals, etc.)
- mold
- towel
- hair dryer
- fork
- decorating supplies (optional)

1
Put the shredded paper in the bowl. Add enough water to cover the paper. Let the paper soak overnight.

2
Pour the soaked paper and water into the blender. Blend until there are no large pieces of paper left.

3
Pour the **pulp** into the tub. Add small leaves, flower petals, herbs, or other bits of nature.

4

Use the dip & lift method to fill the mold (see page 13). Press more bits of nature onto the **pulp**.

5

Press a towel on the pulp to soak up any extra water. Then blow on each side of the mold with a hair dryer for about five minutes.

6

Gently poke the paper with a fork through the **mesh**. This will loosen the paper from the mesh.

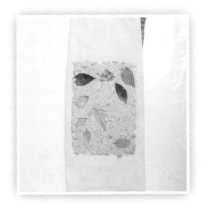

7

Once the paper is free from the mesh, lift the mold off of the paper. Let the paper dry completely. Display your paper as it is, or use decorating supplies to turn it into a card or other craft!

PLANT PAPER

happy harvest

- plant material such as leaves and grasses
- scissors
- measuring cup
- large pot
- water
- strainer
- blender
- plastic tub
- mold
- towel
- hair dryer
- fork
- newspaper
- hair spray
- decorating supplies (optional)

1

Cut the plant material into small pieces. You will need about 3 cups of plant material pieces. Place the plant material in the pot.

2

Add enough water to almost cover the plant material. Let the plant material soak overnight.

3

Have an adult help you use the stove to bring the water to a boil. Boil the plants for one to two hours. The plants and water should turn dark. Turn the stove off and let the plants and water cool.

4

Hold the strainer over the sink. Pour the plant material into the strainer. Then pour the strained material into the blender. Add enough water to cover the plant material.

5

Blend the plant material until there are no large pieces left.

6

Pour the plant **pulp** into the tub.

Continued on the next page.

7

Use the dip & lift method to fill the mold (see page 13).

8

Press a towel on the **pulp** to soak up any extra water. Then blow on each side of the mold with a hair dryer for about five minutes. Keep the towel pressed against the pulp when you turn the mold over.

9

Gently poke the paper with a fork through the **mesh**. This will loosen the paper from the mesh.

10

Once the paper is free from the
mesh, lift the mold off of the paper.
Let the paper dry completely.

11

Once dry, your paper may be
fragile. Spray each side with
hair spray to strengthen it.

happy
harvest

12

Display your paper as it is,
or use decorating supplies
to turn it into a greeting
card or other craft!

PAPIER-MÂCHÉ BOWL

- shredded paper
- bowls
- water
- blender
- strainer
- plastic wrap
- ruler
- newspaper
- paintbrush
- Mod Podge
- acrylic paint

1

Put the shredded paper in the bowl. Add enough water to cover the paper. Let the paper soak overnight.

2

Pour the soaked paper and water into the blender. Blend until there are no large pieces of paper left.

3

Pour the **pulp** into a strainer to remove the extra water.

4
Line a small bowl with plastic wrap.

5
Spread paper **pulp** over the inside of the bowl. Create a layer about ⅛ inch (0.3 cm) thick.

6
Leave the paper pulp in the bowl to dry. This can take several days. When possible, set the bowl in direct sunlight for quicker drying.

7
Set the paper bowl on a sheet of newspaper. Brush Mod Podge over the entire bowl. Let it dry.

8
Paint the bowl. Let it dry.

NOTE:
Your **papier-mâché** bowl should not be used to hold food or liquids.

HANDMADE GIFT BAG

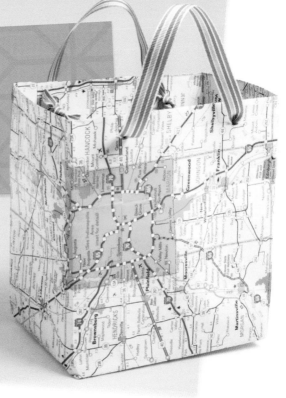

- large sheet of paper (map, sheet music, gift wrap, etc.)
- ruler
- scissors
- marker
- cardboard
- glue stick
- tape
- hole punch
- ribbon

1
Cut a paper rectangle that is 15½ by 8¼ inches (39 by 21 cm).

2
Lay the paper on the table with a long edge at the top. The facedown side will be the outside of the bag.

3
Draw a dotted line across the paper 1¼ inches (3 cm) from the top edge.

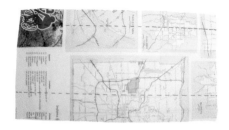

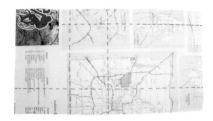

4

Draw a dotted line across the paper 2 inches (5 cm) from the bottom edge.

5

Draw two dotted lines down the paper. The first should be 4½ inches (11 cm) from the left edge. The second should be 7½ inches (19 cm) from the left edge.

6

Draw two more dotted lines down the paper. The first should be ½ inch (1.3 cm) from the right edge. The second should be 3½ inches (9 cm) from the right edge.

7

Fold the paper along each of the dotted lines. Fold them one at a time. Unfold each one before folding the next. Then unfold the paper completely.

8

Cut two strips of cardboard. They should each be 1 by 4¼ inches (2.5 by 10.8 cm).

Continued on the next page.

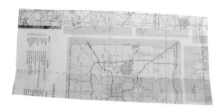

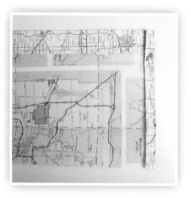

9

Place the strips of cardboard on the paper ¼ inch (0.6 cm) from the top in the sections that are 4½ inches (11 cm) wide. Glue the cardboard in place.

10

Spread glue across the top edge of the paper, including on top of the cardboard pieces. Fold the top edge over. The cardboard strips should be inside the fold.

11

Fold the right edge over, creating a flap. Spread glue on the flap.

12

Bring the left edge over to the right edge. Press the inside of the left edge to the glued flap on the right edge. Let the glue dry.

13

Set the bag on the table with the folded edge down. Fold the tops of the long sides toward each other to form the bottom of the bag.

14

Turn the bag over. Put tape along the bottom seam inside the bag.

15
Turn the bag back over. Fold the bottom corners toward each other. Glue them to the bottom of the bag.

16
Cut another rectangle out of cardboard. Make it 4¼ by 3 inches (10.8 by 7.5 cm).

17
Glue the cardboard rectangle inside the bottom of the bag. This strengthens the bag so it can hold more weight.

18
Punch two holes near the top of the back on one of the long sides. The holes should be about 1 inch (2.5 cm) in from each end of the bag.

19
Cut a ribbon about 10 inches (25 cm) long. Push one end of the ribbon through each hole in the bag from the outside. Tie a knot in each end inside the bag.

20
Repeat steps 18 and 19 to add a ribbon to the other side of the bag.

CONCLUSION

Paper has changed a lot since it was first created. Today's mass-produced paper is practical and inexpensive. But craftspeople are still inspired by **traditional** papermaking methods. These methods take time, patience, and skilled hands. But they result in works of art.

As you practice papermaking, experiment with different methods and sources for **pulp**. Find other natural materials to add color to your paper, such as flower petals, orange peels, and vegetable skins. Keep exploring new ways to use handmade paper to create original works of art.

And like a true artist, keep your eyes and ears open for inspiration. Have an adult help you find online videos of master papermakers at work. Try some of their methods. One day, you could be the one showing your paper art to the world!

GLOSSARY

distribute – to position so as to be properly divided and shared throughout an area.

fragile – easily broken or damaged.

mesh – a sheet made of threads or wires woven loosely so there is space between them.

papier-mâché – paper soaked in glue and made into different shapes before drying.

pulp – a soft, moist material prepared from various fibers, such as wood. Pulp is used to make paper.

traditional – relating to beliefs, customs, and stories handed down from one generation to the next.

ONLINE RESOURCES

Booklinks
NONFICTION NETWORK
FREE! ONLINE NONFICTION RESOURCES

To learn more about papermaking, please visit
abdobooklinks.com or scan this QR code. These links
are routinely monitored and updated to provide the most
current information available.

INDEX